I0409275

Introduction

Welcome to "The Coaches' Guide to Digital Domination: Mastering Online Marketing for Explosive Growth." I'm thrilled to embark on this journey with you as we delve into the world of digital marketing and its transformative potential for coaches like yourself.

In today's fast-paced and interconnected world, a strong online presence is not just a luxury; it's a necessity. As a coach, you possess a unique set of skills and insights that have the power to positively impact the lives of countless individuals. However, to make that impact, you need to ensure that your coaching services are visible, accessible, and engaging in the digital realm.

This comprehensive guide is designed to equip you with the strategies, tools, and knowledge you need to not only navigate the digital landscape but to thrive in it. Whether you're a seasoned coach looking to enhance your online presence or a newcomer eager to make your mark, this eBook is tailored to meet your needs.

We'll cover everything from crafting a compelling personal brand to utilizing social media, content marketing, paid advertising, and more.

You'll learn how to connect with your target audience, showcase your expertise, and create a lasting impression that resonates with potential clients.

But this journey is not just about technical know-how; it's also about embracing a mindset of growth, adaptability, and authenticity.

Your journey to digital mastery is a holistic one, blending practical strategies with the core essence of your coaching philosophy.

As you turn the pages of this eBook, envision the impact you can have on individuals seeking guidance, transformation, and personal growth.

Your coaching business has the potential to make a real difference, and by embracing the principles outlined here, you're paving the way for your coaching legacy to flourish in the digital age. Thank you for joining me on this exciting adventure.
Let's embark on this path to digital dominance and unlock the immense possibilities that await you and your coaching business.

With enthusiasm and anticipation,
Suraj Jaiswal

Chapter 1: Building Your Strong Online Foundation

Your online presence as a coach is more critical than ever in today's digital landscape. In this chapter, we'll delve into the essential elements of establishing a robust foundation for your coaching business's success online.

A successful online presence begins with understanding the fundamentals. Your website serves as the virtual storefront for your coaching practice. Craft a professional, user-friendly website that effectively communicates your brand identity and coaching services. Ensure easy navigation, clear calls to action, and a responsive design that adapts seamlessly to various devices.

Personal branding is key. As a coach, your unique identity is your strongest asset. Define your brand values, mission, and vision. Tailor your messaging and content to resonate with your target audience. Highlight your coaching style and expertise to set yourself apart from the competition.

Content is king in the digital realm. Develop a content strategy that positions you as an authority in your coaching niche.

Start a blog or create resources that address your audience's pain points. Share valuable insights, tips, and actionable advice that showcase your expertise. Regularly update your content to keep your audience engaged and informed.

Engaging on social media is crucial. Choose social media platforms aligned with your coaching goals and target audience. Consistently share relevant content, interact with your audience, and participate in meaningful conversations. Social media provides an avenue to showcase your personality, connect with potential clients, and establish credibility.

Lastly, monitor your progress. Utilize web analytics tools to track your website's performance. Monitor metrics such as website traffic, user engagement, and conversion rates. Regularly review these insights to identify areas of improvement and adjust your strategies accordingly.

In summary, building a strong online foundation involves creating a professional website, defining your personal brand, producing valuable content, engaging on social media, and analyzing your progress. These elements collectively form the backbone of your digital presence, setting the stage for the strategies explored in subsequent chapters of this eBook.

Chapter 2: Navigating Social Media Mastery

In the realm of digital marketing, mastering social media is a game-changer for coaches. In this chapter, we'll explore the strategies to effectively navigate and leverage social media platforms to maximize your coaching business's reach and impact.

Selecting the right social media platforms is essential. Identify where your target audience spends their time and tailor your presence accordingly. Platforms like Facebook, Instagram, LinkedIn, and Twitter offer unique opportunities to engage with potential clients.

Engaging content is at the heart of social media success. Create content that resonates with your audience's needs and interests. Share inspiring stories, actionable tips, and relevant industry news. Use a mix of text, images, and videos to keep your content engaging and diverse.

Consistency matters. Develop a content calendar to plan and schedule your posts. Regular posting maintains your visibility and keeps your audience engaged. However, remember that quality is more important than quantity. Each post should provide value and encourage interaction.

Interaction fosters community. Respond promptly to comments, messages, and mentions. Engage in conversations, answer questions, and thank your audience for their support. Building relationships through genuine interactions can lead to loyal followers and potential clients.

Leverage visual content. Images and videos catch the eye and increase engagement. Share behind-the-scenes glimpses of your coaching journey, success stories, and live videos to connect authentically with your audience.

Social media advertising amplifies your reach. Platforms offer targeted advertising options that allow you to reach specific demographics aligned with your coaching niche. Craft compelling ad copy and visuals that highlight the benefits of your coaching services.

Measure and refine. Utilize social media analytics tools to track the performance of your posts and campaigns. Analyze engagement metrics, audience demographics, and conversion rates. This data provides insights into what's working and helps you refine your strategies.

In conclusion, mastering social media involves selecting the right platforms, creating engaging content, maintaining consistency, fostering interaction, leveraging visual elements, utilizing advertising opportunities, and analyzing your efforts. When harnessed effectively, social media becomes a powerful tool for connecting with your audience and expanding your coaching business's reach.

Chapter 3: The Art of Content Marketing

Content marketing is the cornerstone of establishing authority and connecting with your coaching audience online. In this chapter, we'll delve into the art of creating compelling and valuable content that resonates with your target audience.

Developing a Content Strategy: Begin by defining your content objectives. What message do you want to convey, and what goals do you aim to achieve? Outline the topics you'll cover, ensuring they align with your coaching niche and your audience's needs.

Creating Engaging Blog Posts: Craft blog posts that provide actionable insights, answer common questions, and solve your audience's pain points. Your posts should offer real value and position you as a knowledgeable and helpful resource.

Producing Informative Articles and Guides: Expand your content repertoire with informative articles and guides. Dive deeper into specific topics related to coaching, offering in-depth knowledge and practical advice that your audience can apply.

Utilizing Video and Audio Content: Video and audio content adds a dynamic dimension to your content strategy. Consider creating instructional videos, podcast episodes, or webinars that allow you to connect with your audience on a more personal level.

Showcasing Success Stories: Share success stories of your coaching clients. These stories not only highlight your expertise but also provide social proof of your ability to bring about positive change.

Implementing Effective Call to Actions (CTAs): Incorporate strategic CTAs within your content. Whether it's encouraging readers to subscribe to your newsletter, sign up for a webinar, or schedule a consultation, CTAs guide your audience toward the next step.

Optimizing Content for Search Engines: Integrate relevant keywords into your content to enhance its visibility on search engines. Create informative and well-structured content that not only resonates with your audience but also ranks well in search results.

Promoting Your Content: Once you've created valuable content, promote it across your social media platforms, email newsletters, and other relevant channels. Engage with your audience by encouraging comments, shares, and discussions.

Measuring Content Performance: Use analytics tools to track the performance of your content. Monitor metrics such as page views, time on page, social shares, and conversion rates. Analyze this data to refine your content strategy.

In conclusion, content marketing is about creating valuable, informative, and engaging content that establishes your authority, resonates with your coaching audience, and drives meaningful engagement. By crafting content that addresses your audience's needs, you can effectively connect with potential clients and build lasting relationships.

Chapter 4: Unleashing the Potential of Email Marketing

Email marketing remains a powerful tool for coaches to nurture relationships, share valuable insights, and drive client engagement. In this chapter, we'll explore the strategies to harness the potential of email marketing for your coaching business.

Building and Growing Your Email List: Start by creating a compelling opt-in offer, such as a free guide or webinar, to entice visitors to subscribe to your email list. Implement subscription forms on your website and landing pages to capture leads.

Crafting Irresistible Lead Magnets: Develop lead magnets that address your audience's pain points and offer valuable solutions. Your lead magnet should showcase your expertise while providing immediate value to your subscribers.

Creating Impactful Email Campaigns: Segment your email list based on interests, preferences, and behaviors. Craft targeted email campaigns that resonate with specific segments. Share informative content, success stories, and personalized messages.

Crafting Engaging Email Content: Write email content that is concise, engaging, and valuable. Share tips, insights, and advice that help your subscribers overcome challenges and achieve their goals. Use storytelling to connect on a personal level.

Designing Visually Appealing Emails: Create visually appealing email templates that align with your branding. Use images, graphics, and a clear layout to enhance the readability and visual appeal of your emails.

Implementing Effective Call to Actions (CTAs): Include clear and compelling CTAs in your emails. Whether it's directing subscribers to your latest blog post, inviting them to a webinar, or offering a special promotion, CTAs guide them to take action.

Automating Your Email Marketing: Utilize email marketing platforms to set up automated email sequences. Welcome new subscribers, nurture leads, and provide ongoing value through automated drip campaigns.

Measuring Email Performance: Monitor key email metrics such as open rates, click-through rates, and conversion rates. Analyze the data to identify what content resonates most with your subscribers and optimize your campaigns accordingly.

Measuring Email Performance: Monitor key email metrics such as open rates, click-through rates, and conversion rates. Analyze the data to identify what content resonates most with your subscribers and optimize your campaigns accordingly.

Fostering Meaningful Relationships: Build trust and rapport with your subscribers by delivering consistent value. Encourage interaction by inviting them to reply to your emails, ask questions, and share their insights.

In summary, email marketing is a personalized and direct way to connect with your coaching audience. By building a strong email list, crafting engaging content, designing visually appealing emails, and nurturing relationships through strategic campaigns, you can establish a powerful channel for building a loyal client base.

Chapter 5: Maximizing Your Presence with SEO Strategies

Search Engine Optimization (SEO) is a cornerstone of online visibility, ensuring your coaching services are discoverable by potential clients. In this chapter, we'll delve into the strategies to maximize your presence through effective SEO techniques.

Understanding the Basics of SEO: Begin by understanding the fundamental principles of SEO. Learn about keywords, on-page optimization, off-page optimization, and the importance of quality content.

Conducting Keyword Research: Identify relevant keywords that your target audience might use to search for coaching services. Utilize keyword research tools to find high-impact keywords with reasonable search volumes.

Optimizing On-Page Elements: Optimize your website's on-page elements, including titles, meta descriptions, headers, and image alt tags. Incorporate target keywords naturally while ensuring a user-friendly experience.

Creating Valuable Content: Craft high-quality, informative, and valuable content that addresses your audience's questions and needs. Focus on providing solutions and insights that establish your coaching expertise.

Building Quality Backlinks: Develop a backlink strategy to acquire quality, relevant backlinks from reputable sources. Guest posting, collaborations, and sharing valuable content are effective ways to earn backlinks.

Utilizing Local SEO: If you offer coaching services in specific geographical areas, optimize for local SEO. Create a Google My Business profile, collect reviews, and ensure consistent business information across directories.

Monitoring and Analytics: Utilize SEO tools to monitor your website's performance, track keyword rankings, and identify areas for improvement. Regularly review analytics to measure the effectiveness of your SEO efforts

Adapting to Algorithm Changes: Search engine algorithms evolve over time. Stay updated with industry news and adapt your SEO strategies to align with algorithm changes and best practices..

Mobile-Friendly Optimization: Optimize your website for mobile devices, as mobile-friendliness is a ranking factor. Ensure your website is responsive and provides a seamless experience on all devices.

In conclusion, SEO is an integral part of your online marketing strategy that helps potential clients discover your coaching services. By understanding the basics of SEO, conducting keyword research, optimizing on-page elements, creating valuable content, building backlinks, utilizing local SEO, monitoring analytics, adapting to algorithm changes, and prioritizing mobile-friendliness, you can enhance your online presence and attract a wider audience.

Chapter 6: The Power of Paid Advertising for Coaches

Paid advertising presents an opportunity to amplify your coaching business's reach and target specific audiences with precision. In this chapter, we'll delve into the strategies and benefits of harnessing the power of paid advertising.

Exploring Facebook and Instagram Ads: Facebook and Instagram offer robust advertising platforms that allow you to reach a highly targeted audience based on demographics, interests, and behaviors. Leverage these platforms to showcase your coaching services.

Crafting Compelling Ad Copy and Visuals: Create ad copy that speaks directly to your audience's pain points and aspirations. Craft a clear and concise message that highlights the benefits of your coaching services. Incorporate attention-grabbing visuals that align with your brand.

Utilizing Ad Formats for Impact: Experiment with different ad formats, including image ads, video ads, carousel ads, and slideshow ads. Each format presents a unique way to showcase your coaching expertise and engage your audience.

Setting Targeting Parameters: Define specific targeting parameters to ensure your ads are seen by the right audience. Segment your audience based on factors such as age, gender, location, interests, and behaviors.

Monitoring and Optimizing Ad Performance: Regularly monitor your ad campaigns' performance metrics, including click-through rates, conversion rates, and cost per conversion. Use this data to optimize your campaigns for maximum effectiveness.

Retargeting for Increased Conversions: Implement retargeting strategies to reconnect with individuals who have interacted with your website or content before. Retargeting keeps your coaching services top-of-mind and encourages conversions.

A/B Testing for Refinement: Run A/B tests to experiment with different ad elements such as headlines, visuals, and calls to action. This iterative process helps you identify what resonates most with your audience and refine your ads accordingly.

Budgeting and Scaling Strategies: Allocate your advertising budget wisely and strategically. As you gather data on what works, consider scaling successful campaigns to reach a larger audience and maximize your impact.

Understanding Ad Policies and Guidelines: Familiarize yourself with the advertising policies and guidelines of the platforms you're using. Adhere to these guidelines to ensure your ads are approved and maintain a professional reputation.

In summary, paid advertising offers a targeted and impactful way to reach potential clients and promote your coaching services. By exploring Facebook and Instagram ads, crafting compelling ad copy and visuals, utilizing various ad formats, setting precise targeting parameters, monitoring and optimizing ad performance, implementing retargeting strategies, conducting A/B tests, managing budgets, and adhering to ad policies, you can harness the power of paid advertising to achieve your coaching business goals.

Chapter 7: Personal Branding and Thought Leadership

Establishing a strong personal brand and thought leadership presence is essential for coaches looking to stand out and build lasting connections. In this chapter, we'll explore the strategies to position yourself as a thought leader in your coaching niche.

Positioning Yourself as a Thought Leader: Identify your unique perspective and expertise within your coaching niche. Share valuable insights, research, and opinions that showcase your depth of knowledge and experience.

Crafting Your Personal Brand Identity: Define your personal brand by clarifying your values, mission, and goals. Create a cohesive and authentic online presence that reflects your coaching philosophy and resonates with your audience.

Consistent Content that Demonstrates Authority: Produce consistent, high-quality content that showcases your expertise. Share articles, videos, and webinars that offer valuable insights and actionable advice to your audience.

Leveraging Speaking Engagements and Webinars:
Participate in speaking engagements, workshops, and webinars to share your knowledge with a broader audience. These platforms provide opportunities to connect directly with potential clients.

Engaging on Social Media as a Thought Leader:
Use social media to share your expertise, engage in meaningful discussions, and provide valuable resources to your audience. Be authentic and consistent in your interactions.

Building Authentic Relationships: Foster genuine connections with your audience and peers in your coaching niche. Engage in conversations, respond to comments, and build a supportive community around your brand.

Creating Compelling Thought Leadership Content: Develop thought-provoking content that challenges conventional thinking and offers fresh perspectives. Dive into industry trends, share case studies, and provide actionable strategies.

Collaborating with Industry Influencers:
Collaborate with influencers and experts in your field to expand your reach and credibility. Joint webinars, interviews, and co-authored content can showcase your expertise to a wider audience.

Showcasing Your Journey and Success: Share your personal journey and success stories to inspire others. Transparency about your own challenges and growth can resonate with your audience and build trust.

Incorporating Visual and Design Elements: Use consistent visual elements in your personal brand, such as a recognizable logo, color palette, and imagery. Visual consistency enhances your brand recognition and professionalism.

In conclusion, personal branding and thought leadership are essential for coaches to differentiate themselves and establish a reputation as experts in their niche. By positioning yourself as a thought leader, crafting a cohesive personal brand identity, consistently sharing authoritative content, engaging in speaking engagements and webinars, building authentic relationships, creating compelling thought leadership content, collaborating with influencers, showcasing your journey, and incorporating visual elements, you can solidify your status as a respected authority in the coaching world.

Chapter 8: Measuring and Enhancing Your Digital Success

In the world of digital marketing, continuous improvement is key to achieving your coaching business goals. In this chapter, we'll explore the strategies to effectively measure and enhance your digital marketing success.

Understanding the Importance of Analytics: Analytics provide valuable insights into the performance of your digital marketing efforts. They help you understand what's working, what needs improvement, and where to focus your resources.

Key Metrics to Monitor: Identify the key metrics that align with your goals. Common metrics include website traffic, conversion rates, engagement rates, click-through rates, social media reach, and email open rates.

Interpreting Data for Optimization: Regularly review your analytics data to identify patterns, trends, and areas for improvement. Use this data-driven approach to refine your strategies and make informed decisions.

Using Google Analytics for Website Insights:
Utilize Google Analytics to gain insights into your website's performance. Track user behavior, page views, time on site, and conversion paths to understand how visitors interact with your content.

Tracking Social Media Engagement: Monitor engagement metrics on your social media platforms. Track likes, shares, comments, and clicks to gauge the effectiveness of your social media content and identify trends.

Measuring Email Campaign Performance: Analyze email campaign metrics such as open rates, click-through rates, and conversion rates. Use A/B testing to optimize subject lines, content, and CTAs for better results.

Conversion Tracking and Attribution: Implement conversion tracking to measure specific actions that lead to desired outcomes, such as signing up for a webinar or scheduling a consultation. Understand attribution models to allocate credit to various touchpoints in the customer journey.

Continuous Learning and Adaptation: Stay updated with industry trends, algorithm changes, and emerging technologies. Embrace a mindset of continuous learning and adapt your strategies to stay relevant in the evolving digital landscape.

Optimizing User Experience (UX): Enhance user experience on your website by analyzing user behavior. Ensure easy navigation, fast loading times, and responsive design to keep visitors engaged.

Feedback and Iteration: Encourage feedback from your audience and clients. Use their insights to refine your strategies and content. Embrace an iterative approach that involves testing, learning, and adapting.

In conclusion, measuring and enhancing your digital success requires a strategic approach to analytics and continuous improvement. By understanding the importance of analytics, monitoring key metrics, interpreting data, using tools like Google Analytics, tracking social media engagement, measuring email campaign performance, understanding conversion tracking and attribution, embracing continuous learning, optimizing user experience, and incorporating feedback, you can refine your digital marketing strategies for optimal results.

Chapter 9: Recommended Tools, Platforms, and Resources

To excel in the world of digital marketing, utilizing the right tools and resources is essential. In this chapter, we'll explore a selection of recommended tools, platforms, and resources that can enhance your coaching business's online presence and success.

Essential Digital Marketing Tools for Coaches:

- Google Analytics: Gain insights into your website's performance and user behavior.
- Hootsuite or Buffer: Manage and schedule social media posts across multiple platforms.
- Mailchimp or ConvertKit: Create and manage email marketing campaigns.
- Canva: Design graphics, visuals, and social media posts.
- Keyword Research Tools: Use tools like Google Keyword Planner to identify relevant keywords for your content.

Chapter 9: Recommended Tools, Platforms, and Resources

To excel in the world of digital marketing, utilizing the right tools and resources is essential. In this chapter, we'll explore a selection of recommended tools, platforms, and resources that can enhance your coaching business's online presence and success.

Essential Digital Marketing Tools for Coaches:

- Google Analytics: Gain insights into your website's performance and user behavior.
- Hootsuite or Buffer: Manage and schedule social media posts across multiple platforms.
- Mailchimp or ConvertKit: Create and manage email marketing campaigns.
- Canva: Design graphics, visuals, and social media posts.
- Keyword Research Tools: Use tools like Google Keyword Planner to identify relevant keywords for your content.

Platforms for Streamlining Your Online Presence:

- WordPress: Build a professional and customizable website or blog.
- LinkedIn: Network and share valuable insights within your coaching niche.
- YouTube: Create video content to connect with your audience visually.
- Podcasting Platforms: Share audio content to engage with listeners on a deeper level.
- Webinar Platforms: Host webinars to showcase your expertise and interact with participants.

Valuable Resources for Continued Learning and Growth:

- HubSpot Academy: Access free courses on various digital marketing topics.
- Moz: Learn about SEO through their educational resources and guides.
- Social Media Examiner: Stay updated on social media trends and best practices.
- Digital Marketing Blogs: Follow reputable blogs such as Neil Patel, Content Marketing Institute, and Copyblogger.
- Online Communities: Join forums and groups related to digital marketing and coaching to learn from peers.

Conclusion:

Incorporating these tools, platforms, and resources into your digital marketing strategy can enhance your coaching business's online presence, effectiveness, and impact. By leveraging the right tools, utilizing the power of various platforms, and continuously learning from valuable resources, you can stay at the forefront of the dynamic digital marketing landscape

Chapter 10: Taking Action and Achieving Digital Mastery

In the journey to digital mastery as a coach, taking consistent action is paramount. In this concluding chapter, we'll explore the mindset and steps required to turn the insights from this eBook into tangible results for your coaching business.

Embracing a Growth Mindset:

- Cultivate a mindset of continuous learning and improvement.
- Embrace challenges as opportunities for growth and learning.
- Stay open to experimenting with new strategies and approaches.
- Seek feedback and adapt based on results.

Setting Clear Goals:

- Define specific and measurable goals for your digital marketing efforts.
- Break down your goals into actionable steps and milestones.
- Keep your goals aligned with your overall coaching business objectives.

Creating an Action Plan::

- Develop a detailed action plan for implementing the strategies outlined in this eBook.
- Prioritize tasks and allocate time for each aspect of your digital marketing strategy.
- Create a content calendar to guide your content creation and distribution

Staying Consistent:

- Consistency is key to building a strong online presence.
- Set a consistent schedule for posting content, engaging on social media, and sending emails.
- Over time, your consistency will build trust with your audience.

Monitoring and Iterating:

- Continuously monitor your digital marketing efforts using analytics tools.
- Analyze the performance of different strategies and tactics.
- Use data-driven insights to refine and improve your approach.

Seeking Support and Collaboration:

- Don't hesitate to seek support from mentors, peers, or professionals.
- Collaborate with others in your industry to leverage each other's strengths.
- Join online communities and attend networking events to expand your reach.

Celebrating Success and Learning from Challenges:

- Acknowledge and celebrate your achievements and milestones.
- Learn from any challenges or setbacks you encounter.
- Use both successes and failures as opportunities to grow and refine your approach.

Conclusion:

Taking action and achieving digital mastery as a coach requires dedication, effort, and a willingness to adapt. By embracing a growth mindset, setting clear goals, creating an action plan, staying consistent, monitoring and iterating, seeking support, collaborating, celebrating successes, and learning from challenges, you can navigate the dynamic digital landscape with confidence and drive.

Congratulations on your journey to mastering digital marketing for your coaching business.

The insights and strategies in this eBook are your roadmap to success. **Keep learning, keep evolving, and continue to make a positive impact on the lives of your clients through your coaching expertise.**

Acknowledgments and Contact Information

Before we conclude this eBook, I'd like to extend my gratitude to you for taking the time to delve into the world of digital marketing for coaches. Your dedication to enhancing your coaching business's online presence and impact is truly commendable.

If you have any questions, need further assistance, or would like to discuss any aspect of the content provided in this eBook, please don't hesitate to reach out.

Your success is important, and I'm here to support you on your journey.

Unlock Your Digital Marketing Potential with My Expertise

I'm Suraj Jaiswal, and I'm here to share over a decade of digital marketing wisdom with you. As someone who has spent years navigating the dynamic landscape of digital marketing,

I understand the challenges and opportunities that come with staying ahead in this ever-evolving field. I'm thrilled to offer my expertise through a range of specialized services tailored to enhance your online presence, boost conversions, and drive your digital success to new heights.

My Services: Your Path to Digital Dominance

1. **Strategic Facebook Ad Mastery:** Let's dive into the world of Facebook ads and discover how to craft campaigns that captivate and convert. With my guidance, we'll ensure your ads hit the right targets and deliver a significant return on your investment.
2. **Unleash the Power of Funnels:** Funnels are the backbone of digital success. Together, we'll create funnels that transform casual visitors into engaged customers. Expect a strategic journey that maximizes every touchpoint.

- **Compelling Content Creation:** Content is the beating heart of digital marketing. Let me show you how to create content that resonates, whether it's engaging blog posts, captivating visuals, or impactful social media content.
- **Email Marketing Excellence:** Don't underestimate the power of email. I'll guide you in crafting email campaigns that resonate, build relationships, and drive results through smart segmentation and irresistible content.
- **Crafting Your Digital Identity:** Let's establish your digital brand as a true thought leader. We'll work on personal branding that sets you apart, crafting an identity that reflects your expertise and positions you as a go-to expert.
- **Customized Digital Strategy Consulting:** Need a digital roadmap? I'm here to provide personalized consulting sessions. Together, we'll analyze your current strategies and devise a roadmap that aligns with your unique goals.
- **Engaging Workshops and Webinars:** Join me in interactive workshops and webinars where we'll delve deep into digital marketing strategies. Let's connect with like-minded individuals, learn from each other, and grow together.

Let's Elevate Your Digital Journey

If you're seeking to enhance your digital marketing prowess and elevate your business to new heights, I'm here to guide you. With more than a decade of hands-on experience, I understand the nuances and intricacies of the digital landscape.

Connect with me to start our journey together.

Feel free to reach out through the following channels:

Email: **hello@surajjaiswal.com**

Website: www.surajjaiswal.com

Phone: (+91) 800-2829-800

I look forward to collaborating with you and helping you achieve digital dominance. Together, **let's unleash the full potential of digital marketing and carve a path to success.**

Best regards,
Suraj Jaiswal

www.ingramcontent.com/pod-product-compliance
Lightning Source LLC
Chambersburg PA
CBHW072225290526
45794CB00007B/2895